THE
Picture Guide
TO
Playing
Guitar

WISE PUBLICATIONS
London/New York/Paris/Sydney/Copenhagen/Madrid

Exclusive Distributors:
Music Sales Limited
8/9 Frith Street,
London W1V 5TZ, England.

Music Sales Pty Limited
120 Rothschild Avenue
Rosebery, NSW 2018,
Australia.

Order No.AM952952
ISBN 0-7119-7299-0
This book © Copyright 1998 by Wise Publications

Written by Arthur Dick
Edited by James Sleigh
Photographs by George Taylor
Book design by Chloë Alexander

Printed in the United Kingdom by
Printwise (Haverhill) Limited, Suffolk.

Your Guarantee of Quality
As publishers, we strive to produce every book to the highest
commercial standards. The music has been freshly engraved and
the book has been carefully designed to minimise awkward page
turns and to make playing from it a real pleasure. Particular care
has been given to specifying acid-free, neutral-sized paper made
from pulps which have not been elemental chlorine bleached.
This pulp is from farmed sustainable forests and was produced
with special regard for the environment. Throughout, the printing
and binding have been planned to ensure a sturdy, attractive
publication which should give years of enjoyment. If your copy
fails to meet our high standards, please inform us and we will
gladly replace it.

Music Sales' complete catalogue describes thousands of titles and
is available in full colour sections by subject, direct from
Music Sales Limited. Please state your areas of interest and send a
cheque/postal order for £1.50 for postage to: Music Sales Limited,
Newmarket Road, Bury St. Edmunds, Suffolk IP33 3YB.

Contents

Introduction

So you have your first guitar, you've taken it out of the case, and you want to play your first chords – this book will help you learn the five most commonly used guitar chords. By the end of the book you will be able to play four famous songs by some of the world's greatest recording artists – including The Beatles and Chuck Berry.

You don't even need to be able to read music – all you have to do is copy the chord shapes a finger at a time. At every stage chord shapes and hand positions are indicated clearly with diagrams and photographs – simply look and learn!

Steel string acoustic

Nylon string acoustic

headstock

tuning pegs

nut

frets

fingerboard

neck

body

sound hole

saddle

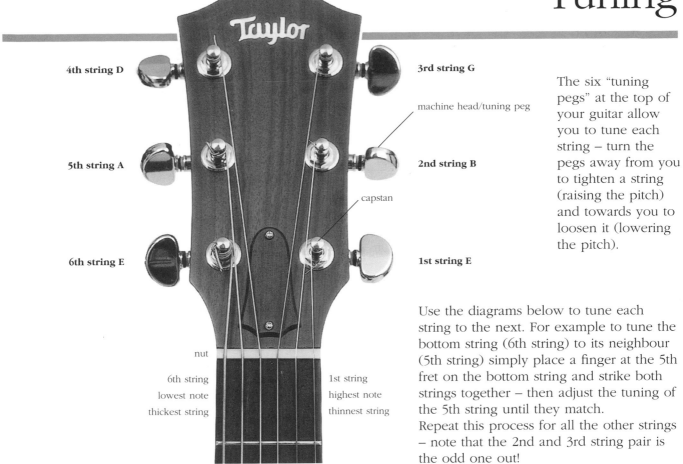

4th string D

3rd string G

machine head/tuning peg

5th string A

2nd string B

capstan

6th string E

1st string E

The six "tuning pegs" at the top of your guitar allow you to tune each string – turn the pegs away from you to tighten a string (raising the pitch) and towards you to loosen it (lowering the pitch).

nut

6th string
lowest note
thickest string

1st string
highest note
thinnest string

Use the diagrams below to tune each string to the next. For example to tune the bottom string (6th string) to its neighbour (5th string) simply place a finger at the 5th fret on the bottom string and strike both strings together – then adjust the tuning of the 5th string until they match.
Repeat this process for all the other strings – note that the 2nd and 3rd string pair is the odd one out!

Relative tuning To tune:

| 6th to 5th string | 5th to 4th string | 4th to 3rd string | 3rd to 2nd string | 2nd to 1st string |

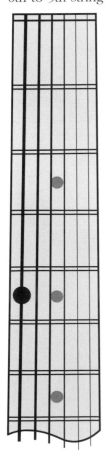
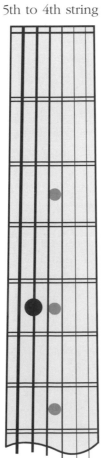

Strings and things

Wind string neatly around machinehead

Of course, there are other ways of tuning your guitar – you could use an electronic tuner, tuning pipes, or even a tuning fork. If you are playing with other people you will need to make sure your guitar is in tune with them.

Caring For The Guitar

Most guitars don't need a great deal of looking after – just make sure that you rub down the strings with a lint-free cloth before you put the guitar back in its case; this will prolong the life of the strings and prevent damage from sweaty hands!

Strings and Re-stringing

Acoustic guitars can be strung with either metal or nylon strings, but all electric guitars have metal ones. Inevitably, at some point in the life of your guitar, you will need to change the strings – either because a string has broken or because they have become dull or tarnished. Make sure you buy a replacement set of strings of the same gauge and take care as you wind the new string round the machinehead.

In reality, there's no right or wrong way to hold your guitar – just check out some of the guitarists on this page to see the wide variety of postures and playing styles. The right posture is the one that feels most comfortable to you. However, for most beginners the playing positions shown below are the best – they'll prevent back pain in the long term and will make it easier to form your first chords on the fretboard.

Strumming

Before you even start to learn your first chord shapes you will need to decide whether or not to strum with a plectrum (or "pick"). The photos below give a "guitarist's-eye-view" of the two strumming styles - with pick and without. Your choice might depend on the sort of music you want to play – folk guitarists often play without a pick, whereas rock players play with one. Experiment with both methods and see which feels most natural to you.

For a beginner, a thick pick will make strumming easier – but once again, try different thicknesses and see which one feels best to you.

Rest your right arm over the body of the guitar, making sure that it is relaxed, and strum gently back and forth over the strings – the movement should be from the elbow. Don't worry about your left hand at this stage – just concentrate on creating an even, rhythmic motion across the strings.

Your left hand is probably already supporting the neck of the guitar – now move it right down to the "nut", keeping the whole arm relaxed. Playing your first chord can be a painful experience – use your thumb behind the neck to support your hand, making sure that your other fingers are not exerting too much pressure.

Relax your whole arm and
let your hand brush across
the strings as it falls.

Your first chord **A Major**

The first chord you're going to learn is called A major – because the major chords are so common they're generally referred to by their letter name only – so this chord is simply called "A".

Place your fingers one at a time making sure that each string sounds clearly. Check the final chord shape as shown below – make sure that your hand position looks the same as the photos.

Once you have mastered the whole shape, pick across each of the six strings, checking that they are all ringing clearly. If the top string is not sounding properly, check your left hand to make sure that you are not inadvertently catching your third finger against it.

The number in the circle tells you which left hand finger to use.

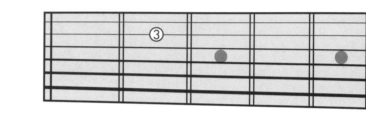

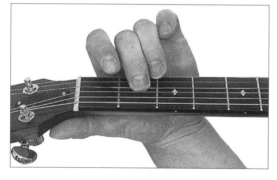

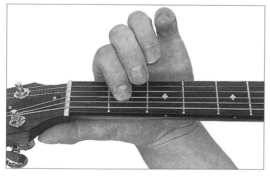

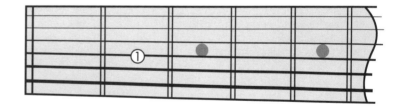

Final chord shape

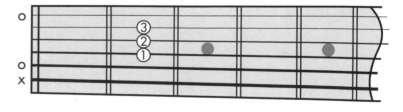

X = don't play this string   **O** = open string

Not all guitar chords use all six strings – to play this chord properly you only need to strum five of them. Although the chord of A sounds fine when all six strings are played, it sounds better if the bottom string is omitted.

This is primarily a problem for your strumming hand – practise by placing your pick (or thumb and first finger) on the fifth string and strumming from there. Gradually you will learn to target the strings you want to hit and avoid those that don't sound good.

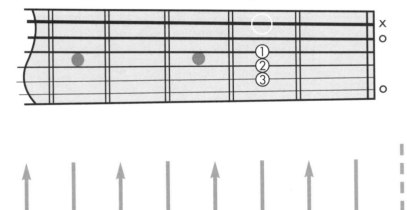

Avoid striking the bottom string

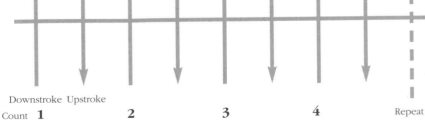

Downstroke Upstroke

Count **1**   **2**   **3**   **4**   Repeat sequence

Now practise strumming up and down rhythmically while holding down the chord of A. Try to strum up and down with a regular, even motion as you count steadily from 1 to 4 – this is what musicians refer to as the "beat". Each down strum should fall on the beat, while the up strums occur between the beats. It's vital to be able to play in time with the beat – especially if you ever want to play in a band.

A new chord **D**

Now try another major chord – this shape is known as D major or simply D. Once again this shape uses three fingers – place them one at a time on the fretboard and check that each string is sounding clearly.

Don't press down too hard with the fingers of your left hand – you'll be surprised how little pressure it actually takes to fret a chord successfully. Positioning your thumb comfortably behind the neck can be helpful.

The number in the circle tells you which left hand finger to use.

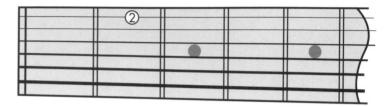

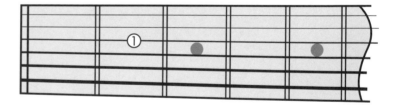

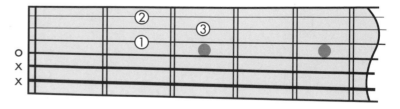

Final chord shape

X = don't play this string   O = open string

This time you only need to strum the top four strings to make the chord of D – the bottom two strings should be avoided – they won't sound good!

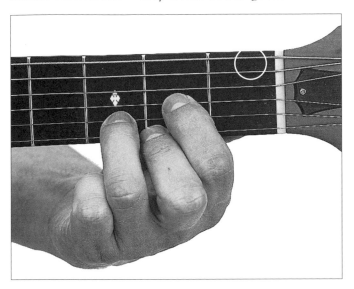

You have now learnt two of the most common chords in pop – A and D. These two chords sound great when played one after the other – you'll find this chord change in hundreds of classic songs.

Avoid striking the bottom 2 strings

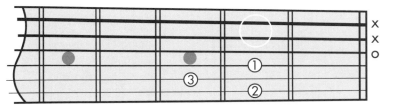

Now practise A to D

You might find moving from the A shape to the D shape slightly tricky – start strumming very slowly (but rhythmically), allowing yourself plenty of time to make the change. The most important thing is to keep in time – it doesn't matter how slowly you play to start with – you can always speed up later.

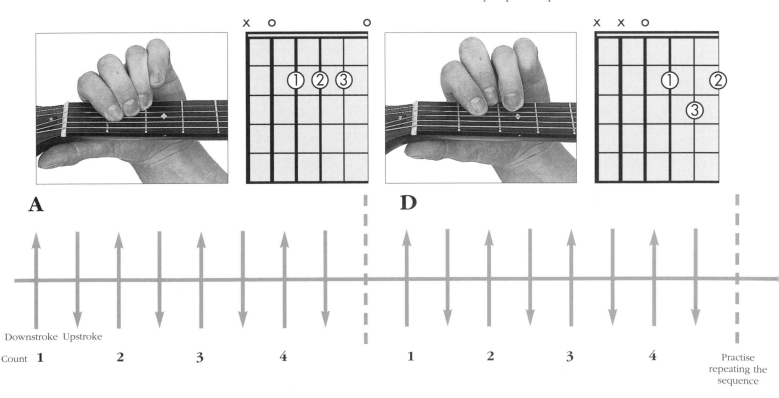

A

D

Downstroke Upstroke

Count   **1**   **2**   **3**   **4**   **1**   **2**   **3**   **4**   Practise repeating the sequence

Your first song **Memphis Tennessee**

Armed with the chords of A and D, you're now ready to tackle a Chuck Berry classic!

This rock'n'roll tune only uses those two chords – try and make sure you change between them as smoothly as possible.

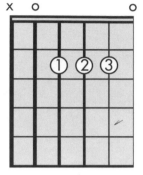

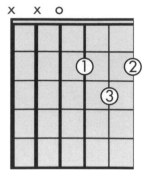

Memphis Tennessee

Words & Music by Chuck Berry

Intro | **D** | **D** | **D** | **D** ‖

Verse 1
    A
Long distance information give me Memphis Tennessee,

Help me find the party tryin' to get in touch with me.
    D
She could not leave her number

But I know who placed the call
       A   **D**
'Cause my uncle took the message and he wrote it on the wall.

Verse 2
    A
Help me information get in touch with my Marie,

She's the only one who'd phone me here from Memphis Tennessee.
    D
Her home is on the south side,

High upon a ridge,
A   **D**
Just a half a mile from the Mississippi Bridge.

Instrumental | **A** | **A** | **A** | **A** |

| **D** | **D** | **A** | **A** **D** | **D** ‖

Verse 3

A
Help me information, more than that I cannot add,

Only that I miss her and all the fun we had,
D
But we were pulled apart

Because her Mom did not agree
A   **D**
And tore apart our happy home in Memphis Tennessee.

Verse 4

A
The last time I saw Marie she's waving me goodbye

With hurry-home drops on her cheek that trickled from her eye,
D
Marie is only six years old,

Information please,
A   **D**
Try to put me through to her in Memphis Tennessee.

A new chord **E**

Here is possibly the most commonly used guitar chord of all time – E major. Just like A and D, the E shape uses three fingers, but this time you can safely strum all six strings.

Try and make sure your left hand fingers arch over to form a right angle with the fretboard – this will ensure that you don't catch adjacent strings. Place your fingers one at a time, following the diagrams below, then strum the final shape, making sure all six strings sound clearly.

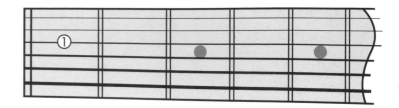

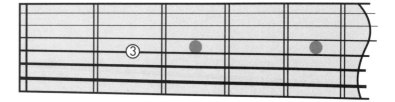

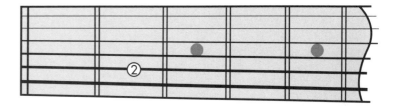

Final chord shape

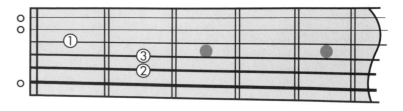

X = don't play this string   **O** = open string

Now practise changing from A to E – strum four beats of each chord, counting steadily. Try and make the transition for A to E (and back again) as smooth as possible.

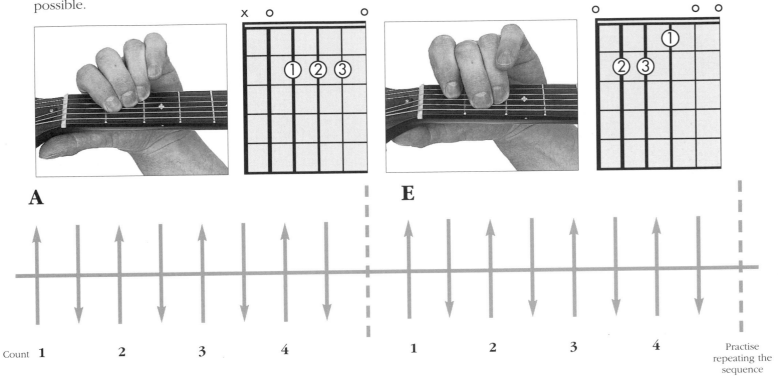

A   **E**

Count **1**   **2**   **3**   **4**   **1**   **2**   **3**   **4**   Practise repeating the sequence

Now it's time to combine all three chords that you have learnt so far. Strum four beats of each chord, counting steadily all the time.

Try thinking ahead to the next chord shape as you strum, so that you are ready to change shape after the fourth beat.

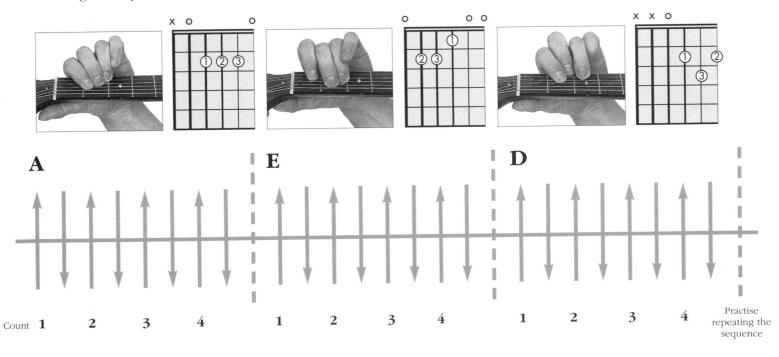

A   **E**   **D**

Count **1**   **2**   **3**   **4**   **1**   **2**   **3**   **4**   **1**   **2**   **3**   **4**   Practise repeating the sequence

Your next song Love Me Do

The verse of the first Beatles hit single will provide you with another chance to practise changing from A to D, while the bridge section introduces the chord of E.

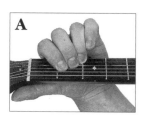
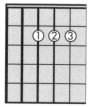
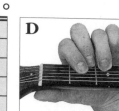

Love Me Do

Words & Music by John Lennon & Paul McCartney

Intro	| **A**	| **D**	| **A**	| **D**	|
	| **A**	| **D**	| **A**	| **A**	||

Verse 1

  A   **D**
Love, love me do,
      A   **D**
You know I love you,
    A   **D**
I'll always be true,

So please_____
        A **D** **A**   **D**
Love me do, oh   love me do.

Verse 2

  A   **D**
Love, love me do,
      A   **D**
You know I love you,
    A   **D**
I'll always be true,

So please _____
        A **D** **A**
Love me do, oh love me do.

Bridge

  E
Someone to love,
D   **A**
Somebody new,
  E
Someone to love,
D   **A**
Someone like you.

Verse 3

  A   **D**
Love, love me do,

    A   **D**
You know I love you,

    A   **D**
I'll always be true,

So please_____

      A D A
Love me do, oh love me do.

Instrumental ‖: **E** | **E** | **D** | **A**   :‖ *Repeat this sequence*

| **A** | **A** | **A** | **A**   ‖

Verse 4

  A   **D**
Love, love me do,

    A   **D**
You know I love you,

    A   **D**
I'll always be true,

So please _____

      A D A   **D**
Love me do, oh love me do.

Coda

     A
Yeah, love me do,

D   **A**   **D**
Woh-oh love me do.   *(Fade)*

A new chord **C Major**

This is chord is slightly more difficult than the three you have already learnt, because an open string is hidden in the middle of the chord shape.

Be careful not to catch the open third string with your second finger, and similarly, don't muffle the open top string with your first finger.

Once again, if you attempt to make your fingers meet the fingerboard at right angles you shouldn't have any problems.

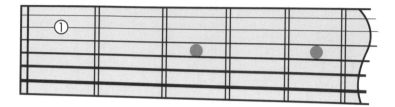

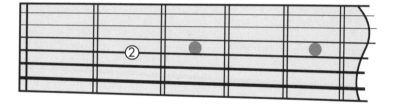

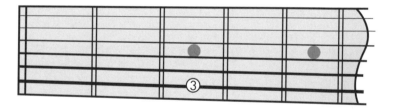

Final chord shape

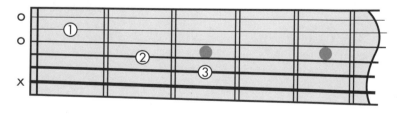

X = don't play this string   **O** = open string

As with the chord of A, C major will sound much better if you avoid strumming the bottom string.

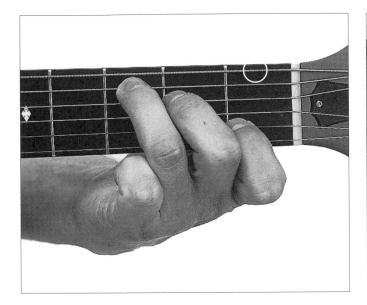

Now try practising a change from C to D to A. Allow yourself plenty of time to change between the different shapes, while maintaining a steady beat.

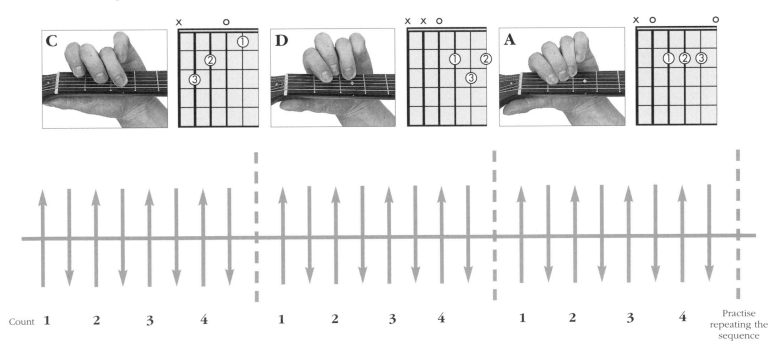

| Count | 1 | 2 | 3 | 4 | 1 | 2 | 3 | 4 | 1 | 2 | 3 | 4 | Practise repeating the sequence |

Your next song Get It On

The chords you have just been practising now come together in this T. Rex classic – Get It On.

A steady rhythmic feel is essential for this glam rocker!

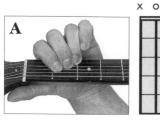  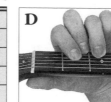 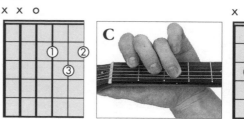 

Get It On

Words & Music by Marc Bolan

Verse 1
        A
Well you're dirty and sweet,
D   **A**
Clad in black, don't look back, and I love you,
D   **A**
You're dirty and sweet, oh yeah.

Well you're slim and you're weak,
       D   **A**
You've got the teeth of the Hydra upon you,
D   **A**
You're dirty sweet and you're my girl.

Chorus 1
   C   **D**   **A**
Get it on, bang a gong, get it on.
   C   **D**   **A**
Get it on, bang a gong, get it on.

Verse 2
        (A)
Well you're built like a car,
       D   **A**
You've got a hubcap diamond star halo,
D   **A**
You're built like a car, oh yeah.

Well you're an untamed youth, that's the truth,
                              D
With your cloak full of eagles
       A
You're dirty sweet and you're my girl.
D   **A**

Chorus 2   As Chorus 1

Verse 3

          A
Well you're windy and wild
            D   **A**
You've got the blues in your shoes and your stockings,
  D   **A**
You're windy and wild, oh yeah.

Well you're built like a car,
        D   **A**
You've got a hubcap diamond star halo,
     D   **A**
You're dirty sweet and you're my girl.

Chorus 3   As Chorus 1

Instrumental ‖: A | A | A | A   :‖ *Repeat this sequence*

Verse 4

         (A)
Well you're dirty and sweet,
     D   **A**
Clad in black, don't look back, and I love you,
   D   **A**
You're dirty and sweet, oh yeah.

Well you dance when you walk,
     D   **A**
So let's dance, take a chance, understand me,
     D   **A**
You're dirty sweet and you're my girl.

Chorus 4 ‖:   **C**   **D**   **A**
           Get it on, bang a gong, get it on. :‖ *Play 3 times*

Instrumental ‖: A | A | A | A   :‖

Chorus 5 ‖:   **C**   **D**   **A**
           Get it on, bang a gong, get it on. :‖ *Play 3 times*
         C   **D**   **A**
Get it on, bang a gong, right on!
        C D A
Take me!

Coda
(spoken)   Well meanwhile I'm still thinkin'.

A new chord **G Major**

The chord of G completes the set of five classic guitar chords that you're going to learn. G is a great-sounding open chord using all six strings.

Once again, care must be taken not to muffle the open fourth and second strings with the fretting fingers.

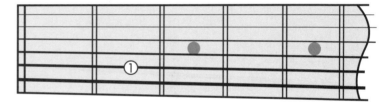

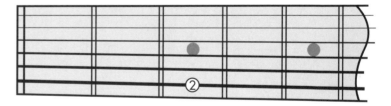

Final chord shape

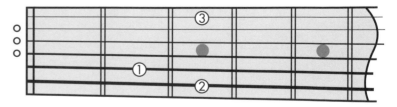

X = don't play this string   **O** = open string

Now practise changing from A to G.

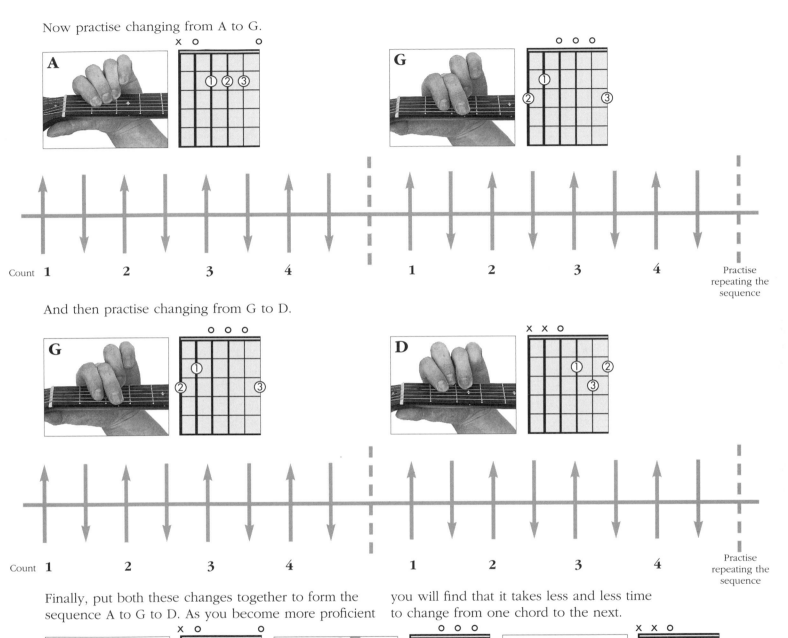

And then practise changing from G to D.

Count **1**   **2**   **3**   **4**   **1**   **2**   **3**   **4**   Practise repeating the sequence

Finally, put both these changes together to form the sequence A to G to D. As you become more proficient you will find that it takes less and less time to change from one chord to the next.

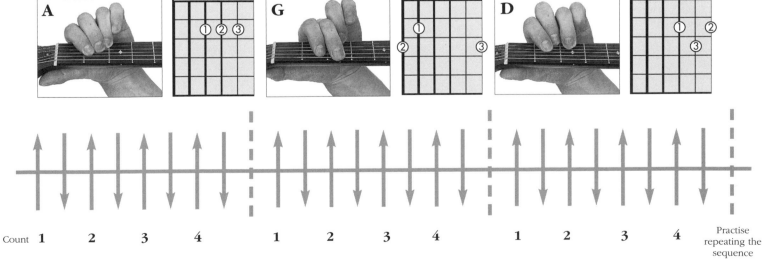

Count **1**   **2**   **3**   **4**   **1**   **2**   **3**   **4**   **1**   **2**   **3**   **4**   Practise repeating the sequence

The Grand Finale **Get Back**

This 1969 Beatles rocker uses the chord sequence you've just been practising. Once again, the verse alternates between the chords of A and D, but look out for the fast change from G to D in the chorus!

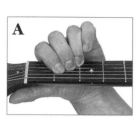
A

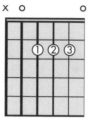

G

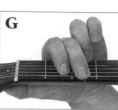

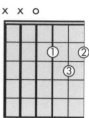
D

Get Back

Words & Music by John Lennon & Paul McCartney

Intro | **A** | **A** | **A** | **A G D** ‖

Verse 1
A
Jo Jo was a man who thought he was a loner
D   **A**
But he knew it couldn't last.

Jo Jo left his home in Tucson, Arizona
D   **A**
For some California grass.

Chorus 1
A   **D**   **A**   **G D**
Get back, get back, get back to where you once belonged,
            A   **D**   **A**
Get back, get back, get back to where you once belonged.

(Get back Jo Jo).

Instrumental | **A** | **A** | **D** | **A G D** ‖

Chorus 2
            A   **D**   **A**   **G D**
Get back, get back, get back to where you once belonged,
            A   **D**   **A**
Get back, get back, get back to where you once belonged.

(Get back Jo).

Instrumental | **A** | **A** | **D** | **A G D** ‖

A
Verse 2   Sweet Loretta Martin thought she was a woman
D   **A**
But she was another man.

All the girls around her say she's got it coming
D   **A**   **G D**
But she gets it while she can.

Chorus 3   As Chorus 1

Instrumental | **A** | **A** | **D** | **A**   **G D** ‖

    A   **D**   **A**   **G D**
Chorus 4   Get back, get back, get back to where you once belonged,
     A   **D**   **A**
Get back, get back, get back to where you once belonged.

(Get back Jo).

    A   **D**
Coda   Get back Loretta,
(spoken)   **A**   **G D**
Your Mommy is waiting for you

                              D
Wearin' her high-heeled shoes and her low neck sweater
          A   **G D**
Get back home Loretta.

Chorus 5   ‖: As Chorus 1 :‖   *Repeat to fade*

The Check List

Armed with the five chords you've learnt in this book, you will now be able to play hundreds of classic rock tracks. Experiment with different strumming patterns and chord sequences, and maybe even try writing some songs of your own!

A

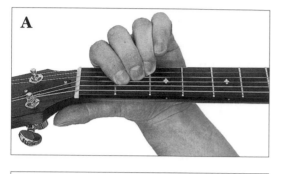
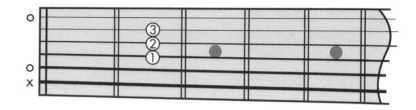

D

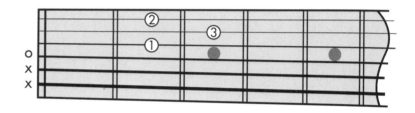

E

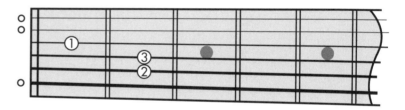

C

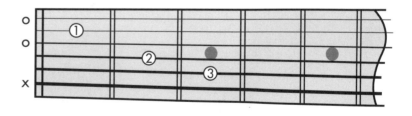

G

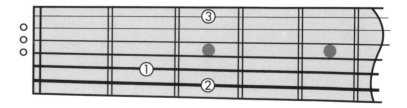

Now take the five chords you've learnt and try these other classic chord sequences:

All Right Now – Free
A, **D**, **G**, **E**

Blue Suede Shoes – Elvis Presley
A, **D**, **E**

Born To Be Wild – Steppenwolf
A, **C**, **D**, **E**

Brimful Of Asha – Cornershop
A, **D**, **E**

Common People – Pulp
G, **C**, **D**

Elephant Stone – The Stone Roses
G, **C**, **D**

Hey Joe – Jimi Hendrix
C, **G**, **D**, **A**, **E**

The Jean Genie – David Bowie
A, **E**, **D**, **G**

Jumping Jack Flash – The Rolling Stones
Verse – **A**, **D**, **G**
Chorus – **C**, **G**, **D**, **A**

Lay Down Sally – Eric Clapton
A, **D**, **E**

Mr Tambourine Man – Bob Dylan
G, **A**, **D**, **G**, **D**, **G**, **A**

Paperback Writer – The Beatles
G, **C**, **D**

Peggy Sue – Buddy Holly
A, **D**, **E**

Shaker Maker – Oasis
Verse – **A**, **D**, **A**, **G**, **D**, **A**

Walk Of Life – Dire Straits
A, **D**, **E**

Some other chords to try out

If this introduction to the world of chords has whetted your appetite, check out some other essential chord shapes:

Remember that not all chords use all six strings - so take care which strings you hit!

A minor

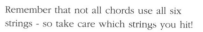

Don't strike the 6th string!

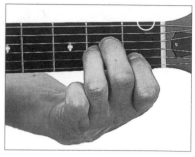

E minor

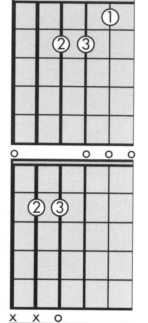

D7

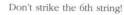

Don't strike the 5th and 6th strings!

E7

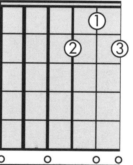

Don't strike the 6th string!

A7

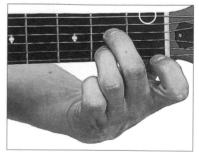

These extra shapes open up new possibilities, as demonstrated by these rock standards:

Imagine – John Lennon
Verse: **G**, **C**, **G**, **C**, **G**, **C**, **G**, **C**
Chorus: **Em**, **Am**, **C**, **D**

All Along The Watchtower – Bob Dylan/ Jimi Hendrix
Em,**C**, **D**

Eleanor Rigby – The Beatles
Em, **C**, **Em**, **C**

Everything Must Go – Manic Street Preachers
Chorus: **E**, **Am**, **D**, **E**

Love Is All Around – Wet Wet Wet
G, **Am**, **C**, **D**

Massachusetts – The Bee Gees
G, **Am**, **C**, **G**

Roll Over Beethoven – Chuck Berry
A7, **D7**, **E7**

Lady Jane – The Rolling Stones
C, **G**, **D**, **E**, **Am**, **D7**

If you're keen to develop your chord playing, why not check out some of the other exciting titles available from Music Sales:

Really Easy Guitar! Series:
The Beatles NO90692
Rock Classics AM957693

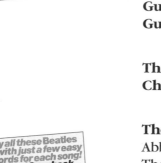

FastForward Series:
Acoustic Guitar Chords AM950940
Blues Guitar AM951160
Blues Guitar Licks AM92451
Fingerpicking Guitar AM951159

First Guitar Chords AM954173

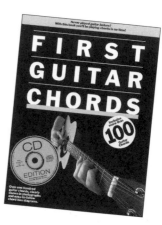

Guitar Chords To Go! AM954173
Guitar Scales To Go! AM954261

**The Complete Guitar Player
Chord Encyclopedia** AM90134

The Chord Songbook Series:
Abba AM959740
The Beatles NO90664
Blur AM936914
Bon Jovi AM936892
Eric Clapton AM956054
The Corrs AM956967
The Cranberries AM944383
Levellers AM951445
Metallica AM944680
Alanis Morissette AM944086
Oasis AM936903
Oasis Be Here Now AM950763
Pulp AM942678
Stereophonics AM956065
Sting AM940489
Stone Roses AM951490
Paul Weller AM942546
Wet Wet Wet AM938135

These books, and many more, are available from all good music retailers
(quoting order numbers above) or, in case of difficulty, contact
Music Sales Limited, Newmarket Road, Bury St. Edmunds, Suffolk IP33 3YP.
Telephone 01284 725725; Fax 01284 702592.
www.musicsales.com

If you would like copies of Music Sales' full-colour catalogues, see page 2 for details.